REDEFINING OUR RELATIONSHIPS
GUIDELINES FOR RESPONSIBLE OPEN RELATIONSHIPS
WENDY-O MATIK

DEFIANT TIMES
PRESS
Oakland, CA

ISBN-10: 1-58790-015-7   ISBN-13: 978-1-58790-015-0

Graphic design by Eve
Cover art & illustrations by Erin Brookey
Back cover photo by Karoline Collins
Logo design by Anna Brown
Special thanks to 1984 Printing, Regent Press, Iconography Press

Defiant Times Press
Oakland, CA
www.wendyomatik.com

All contents of this book are true and lived experiences; names
have been changed.

Library of Congress Cataloging-in-Publication Data

Matik, Wendy-O, 1966-
    Redefining our relationships : guidelines for responsible open
    relationships / Wendy-O Matik.
        p. cm.
    ISBN 1-58790-015-7
    1. Interpersonal relations. I. Title.

HM1106 .M38 2002
302--dc21   2001051971

Printed in the USA

Additional books by Wendy-O Matik:
Damaged Goods, Defiant Times Press (2001)
Gutless, Defiant Times Press (1998)
Love Like Rage, manic d press (1994)
Fill It Full of Holes, Defiant Times Press (1995)
She Knew Better, manic d press (1992)
So Much for Passion, manic d press (1990)

Book Compilations:
Concrete Dreams: Manic D Press Early Works, manic d press (2002)
Revival: Spokenword from Lollapalooza '94, manic d press (1995)
Signs of Life: Channel Surfing Through 90s Culture, manic d press (1994)
Psyche Subversion, Andromeda Press (1992)

Discography:
Total War Against State & Capital, Vol. I, Hidden Power
Enterprises, Sweden (2001)
Krauts, Yanks & Limeys!, Bremen, Oakland, Bath Sampler, GEMA
Records, Germany (1998)
Home Alive: The Art of Self Defense, Epic Records, USA (1996)
Gag Order, *False Faces,* Judgmental Music, USA (1994)
Logical Nonsense/Grimple Split, East Bay Menace Records, USA (1993)
Consolidated, *Play More Music,* Play It Again Sam
Records/Netwerk Europe (1992)
Powerless II: No More Flowers, No More Ribbons, Black Plastic
Records, USA (1992)
Give Me Back, Ebullition Records, USA (1991)
Econochrist, Ebullition Records, USA (1988-1993)

Videography:
*Step Up and Be Vocal, Interviews zu Queer Punk und Feminismus in San
Francisco,* Step Up and Be Vocal, Bremen, Germany (2002)
Gynopunk, University of California Berkeley, Senior Film Project,
USA (May 1994)

The author wishes to extend her deepest heartfelt thank you to Noah, Adrienne, Famous, Erin, and Carey, without whose moral support I could not have stood the weight of the task ahead of me. Your constant encouragement anchored me in my conviction and gave me the strength to believe in myself.

A special thanks to Eve, Mark Weiman, and Markley, as well as the countless people who helped this book into fruition, either in spirit or in actual time and energy.

This book is dedicated to and inspired by each and every person who has touched my life.

"The most vital right is the right to love and be loved."
Emma Goldman

"Our belief is that the human capacity for sex and love and intimacy is far greater than most people think--possibly infinite--and that having a lot of satisfying connections simply makes it possible for you to have a lot more."
Easton and Liszt, The Ethical Slut: A Guide to Infinite Sexual Possibilities

Table of Contents

Definitions

Partner: your primary companion.

Lover: your friend, platonic or sexual. A lover is essentially anyone in your life with whom you care for, respect and maintain a friendship.

Open Relationship: a radically different, re-defined relationship outside the status quo, where partners encourage non-restrictive paths of love while remaining seriously committed to their primary partner(s), friends, and lovers. In theory, open relationships seek a non-hierarchical form of love.

Monogamy: a single-companion relationship be it sexual, romantic, or otherwise.

Jealousy: demanding complete devotion beyond reason; suspicion of a rival or of one believed to enjoy an advantage; distrustfully watchful.

Making Love = Being Loving: anything and everything that you put your heart into, including intercourse, a hand shake, kissing, a love letter, a peace offering, S/M, art, music, masturbation, fetishes, fantasies, a phone call, a warm embrace, whatever pleases you, whatever feels good, the sky is the limit. I dare you to count the ways you can single-handedly make love to the planet or yourself or your best friend or your new lover.

Rule: a mutual agreement, understanding, decision or arrangement.

"Multipartner relationships is seen as this alternative. It combines traditional concepts of commitment, love and "a lifelong intention to support each other in whatever ways seem appropriate" with the more controversial idea of sexually relating to more than one person at the same time with all partners fully aware of this." Lano & Parry, <u>Breaking the Barriers to Desire: New Approaches to Multiple Relationships</u>

Why an Alternative Relationship?

With the encouragement from many friends to write about what I've lived, I have been inspired to take a wild stab into the world of radically defined relationships. I have no role models but my own, as I am currently celebrating over 13 successful years of an alternative relationship. I'll be the first to admit, 'it's no small feat!' My motive for this book was based on the very lack of open discussion on the topic of relationships and love. My aim is merely to incite an inner revolution in the hearts and minds of those who will dare to read this.

I have spent the greater part of my life coming to grips with the fact that I am unable to be monogamous, unable to restrain my heart from loving other people, unable to keep my desires under lock and key. Concepts like "cheating", "betrayal", and "faithfulness to one and only one person" continue to confuse and alienate me. I have always enjoyed different people for different reasons. As a woman who fiercely guards her freedom, I can't imagine being limited by a monogamous relationship where one person must try to fulfill all my needs and desires.

By re-defining my relationship, I have come to learn so much about myself and about my partner. I have learned that in reality, I can't depend on one person be the sole provider of everything I have ever desired in life. No one can be all those things, that's why we have friends and family and that's why we foster nurturing relationships with other people. Other friends and relationships can alleviate the pressure imposed on a primary partner to meet all of one's needs. Expecting my partner to provide all these things is unfair and unrealistic--it sets one up for disappointment when a partner can't meet one's expectations.

I want to make clear from the onset that this book is not about the pros and cons of monogamy versus non-monogamy. I have chosen to write about what I have lived and experienced, open relationships. I strongly believe that open relationships reduce the hazards that accompany unhealthy co-dependency. Open relationships challenge us to confront our jealousy and possessiveness. Committing to a relationship not mapped out by our parents, or society, or Hollywood means tearing down the very foundation of status quo and conformity. It means re-defining and re-building a relationship based on your needs and your values. Loving openly and freely in this day and age is a political act.

Put together your own vision of an ideal relationship, re-sculpt your own belief system, redefine the potential of a friendship, imagine a thousand ways to make love to yourself and anyone you care about. And while you're at it, re-invent your gender, sexual preferences and orientation.

Radicalize your relationship by imagining your wildest ideal partnership together. Avoid stagnancy by challenging your old familiar routine and re-inventing new levels of commitment. Face your true desires in life by asking yourself what you really want from your connections, and then make those desires clear to all those involved, from friends to lovers to partners. Have you ever dreamed of a live-in partner or maybe two? Do you prefer to live alone and have several outside, meaningful relationships where you work out a fair system to spend time with all of them at different times, like you manage to do with your friends? It can be done. If you are skeptical and doubtful that non-monogamy can work, then it won't work. If you believe in the freedom of desires and have the determination to pursue what's in your heart, anything is possible. All partners or lovers must agree on this as a mutual goal for such a relationship to work.

An open relationship allows you to be a better lover to yourself as well as to others. It opens your perception and helps you cope with the reality of human nature, which is to seek out love, to give love, and to receive love over and over again in its many forms and many faces.

One man writes:

"I would like to hear more discussions on the idea that one person cannot fulfill all our needs--it's one of the strongest arguments for non-monogamy for me. There are real virtues and benefits of non-monogamy (not just the logistics of how to do it), such as the personal growth one experiences by letting go of jealousy, knowing that your lover/partner is a freer person because of your understanding, and the fact that all involved have an opportunity to get to know, love, and experience different people."

Intimacy

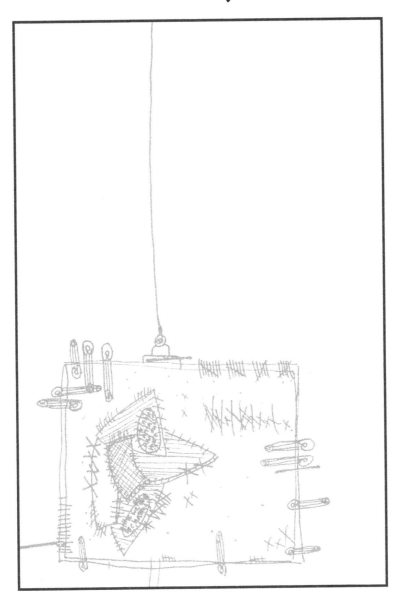

"Love for another does not diminish or alter our love for existing partners. It enhances it. More partners allow us to experience ourselves in different ways and fulfill more of our potentials. We become more integrated and are less likely to resent a monogamous partner because of unmet needs." Paul King, <u>Polyamory: Ethical Non-Monogamy</u>

Intimacy

The widely acclaimed "bible" among most non-monogamists is <u>The Ethical Slut: A Guide to Infinite Sexual Possibilities</u> by Easton and Liszt. I found this book to be a helpful guide in understanding the sexual component in ourselves and in our relationships, managing multiple partners or lovers, and handling jealousy and conflict resolution. For the purposes of this book, I have intentionally de-emphasized the topic of sex, intercourse, or the sexual component of open relationships. My reasons for this are complex and would require another book to make my philosophy on physical love comprehensible. I am asking people to re-invent their common notions of sex, to go beyond the limits of intercourse equating to sex, beyond the physical, expanding one's mind and heart to the enormous and mysterious gray area of intimacy.

Have you ever gotten into one of those mind-blowing, heartfelt, intense discussions with someone, felt your body temperature rise, experienced the exchange of a truly passionate and intimate dialogue and when it was over, you felt as if you had made love to that person? You feel somehow changed, receptive, and bursting with a kind of love for that person that you may not have felt before. Have you ever felt as though you just had "sex" after a romantically succulent meal with someone? Has a hug or a long awaited embrace ever felt like you were falling in love? Have you ever imagined yourself exchanging a kiss that was better than sex, that somehow could convey all the love that you feel in a single ignited moment?

This is the gray area of intimacy of which I am trying to scratch the surface. To give love is a personal and revolutionary act. Everyone I love as a friend or a lover or a sister or a grandmother embodies a form of daily activism in my life. Every love letter, every hug, every tender kiss, every flower picked, every consoling talk is my heart acting out all the love and kindness that overfills me. I have other outlets--gardening, motorcycle riding, cooking, sewing, poetry/spokenword, playing bass, exchanging letters and so on--but my deeper connections with special people give me such an untouchable high and satisfaction. *This* is why I practice and believe in open relationships. It is not sexual validation that I'm searching for, but the mere act of giving, sharing, growing, inspiring, and loving creatively. I almost feel like I could not go on with life without these connections.

An open relationship cannot be reduced to the act of sex alone. There are more than a thousand ways to make love, to re-create intimacy in your every day life, to suck the juices from a piece of fruit and feel full for the first time. Being in an open relationship means you have the revolutionary opportunity to have guilt-free sex with life, with yourself, with your soul. Expand your notions of eroticism, re-discover verbal and written affection, invent a new way to hug that truly expresses how much you feel for that person, massage every inch of your lover's body without making sex the goal.

Above all else, exercise being vulnerable with partners, friends, lovers, and family members. Open up that under-worked heart of yours and tell someone you love how much they mean to you, give them a compliment, stroke their ego, reveal something tender and real about yourself. The odds are that it may not be returned by the one desired individual that you have chose to open up to, but it doesn't mean that it won't come around in another way, by a different means. To give without expecting something in return is the ultimate gift of love, but it takes practice.

Strive to be intimate and loving every day. Here's our list of keeping our love alive and exciting: camping, eating out, barbecue at the beach, arts & craft projects, long scenic drives, video/sound projects, un-birthday parties, kite flying, flowers, gardening, taking pictures of our adventures, watching sunsets, just to name a few.

Make it up as you go along. This is the beauty of re-inventing your own relationship. The benefits of multiple partners or lovers or friends means that you get to experience the different parts of yourself with different people. Re-examine such concepts as betrayal, cheating or unfaithfulness and ask yourself if these still apply to your relationships, how and why. Practice being faithful to all your lovers by respecting them, honoring your commitments to them, and being a good friend to all. It shouldn't surprise you how filled our heads are with Hollywood's preconceived notions of honor and loyalty. It shouldn't surprise you how indoctrinated we all are in patriarchal concepts of possessiveness. If these institutions are not exposed for the tools of inequality that they are, then we will continue to blindly perpetuate them.

"Responsible non-monogamy means a non-monogamous lifestyle or arrangement in which all the partners concerned are aware of and consent to the form of relationship." Lano & Parry, <u>Breaking the Barriers to Desire: New Approaches to Multiple Relationships</u>

Open Relationships

No matter how monogamous one may claim to be, many of us at some point in our life have been non-monogamous in either a one-night-stand or a non-committal relationship for any length of time. Many of us have fondled the idea that even though a new relationship may not unfold into something more serious down the road, it is still significant and worth pursuing. When we are not in a serious relationship, we may bounce around from person to person until we find what we want. Anyone who is skeptical of "open" relationships, can look at their own life for examples of times when seeing more than one person was acceptable and worthwhile. For example, shortly after the break up of a long-term relationship, we may prefer to have one or two casual relationships, or a few short "flings," but nothing too intense.

This is not to imply that we are all non-monogamous by nature. I believe that I am, but it is not for the great majority of people I know. It comes down to personal choice. I am an activist of the heart. My personal revolution guards this right to be openly loving with others. Long before I declared myself "alternative," I knew for certain that I did not think or act or look or feel like the masses around me. Before I knew what conformity or status quo meant, I had the strong inner belief that I was different and that

15

"normal" was something I couldn't relate to.

So began the early pre-teen cognitive process of re-defining everything that affected me personally. Being a non-conformist had less to do with not following the masses and everything to do with mapping out my life for myself, regardless of everybody else's judgments. I remember as early as age nine, I was aware that I was attracted to boys and girls in the same way. If I had let societal norms dictate what I should be, I would have never been able to discover and explore my sexual identity.

"Coming out of the closet" with myself and others about being non-monogamous has been more difficult than coming out as a bisexual person. There are times when you would like to keep your private life priv, but the challenge is not forcing yourself into a world of lie d secrecy. I will explore this issue again in the summary.

Socie will do everything it can to draw restrictive lines around you e--how you should look, how you should feel, what your goal ould be, and what your future should look like. Some of these a'll choose to keep, others you'll discard. But ultimately you ha he choice to define your life and your relationships as you see If you don't honor these choices and the inherent re sibility that comes with them, you'll never know your true t tial.

uestions for yourself

What would an ideal relationship be like for me? Who am I but common and collected desires bound by sociocultural norms? What is a "normal" relationship? What kind of role models do I have for alternative and radical relationships? What are my boundaries, self-imposed or otherwise? What am I scared of?

Misconceptions

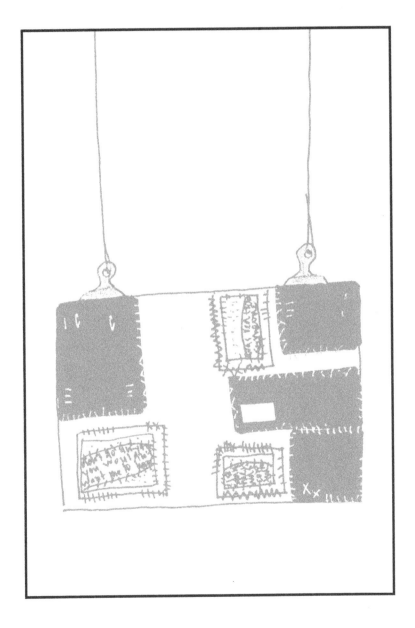

"Monogamous marriage as we know it today is based on patterns established in Biblical times governing men's ownership of women. In Biblical days, the law prescribed that women be stoned to death for taking a lover, but men were allowed as many secondary wives or concubines as they could afford." Dr. Deborah M. Anapol, Polyamory: The New Love Without Limits

Misconceptions

Open relationships are not just about open sex. This seems like an obvious statement to most people who practice radically different relationships, but there are many people who misunderstand what you mean by "open." There are a thousand or more ways to be loving with someone--sex is the easy part. It's being creative enough to actively commit to being a loving person on a multitude of levels (cuddling, holding, listening, love letters, the exchange of inspiration and so on) that separates you from the norm. An open relationship has less to do with sex and everything to do with consent, honesty, consequences, dispelling of feelings of possessiveness, being supportive and communicative. Be aware of your own stereotypes of what an open relationship means. You are free to define your relationship in any way your heart desires, so long as personal respect and integrity are at the core.

Open relationships are a way of life. It is a form of multi-partnerships which encompasses economic, political, social and philosophical alternatives to every day life. Non-monogamy does not equate to marathon sex or sport-fucking or a game by which the person with the most sexual partners wins. Responsible non-monogamy is an expression of the true desires of your heart and a calling in your soul.

Another misconception for those new to open relationships is the issue of commitment. Responsible open relationships require the truest adherence to commitment to the future of any and all relationships. Non-monogamous individuals are not necessarily "swingers" looking for an easy lay or sex without strings. In fact, open relationships do not function at all without all parties involved making a commitment to honesty, communication, patience, and hard work. Non-monogamous partners are simply willing to engage in deeply committed, serious relationships with more than one person (primary, friend, lover, pen pal).

An equally disheartening misconception is the old adage, "intimacy or sex will ruin the friendship." This is certainly true if you haven't established a good foundation of trust and communication with this friend or if you never really had a commitment to the friendship in the first place. Every lover has always been my friend first. If you set out to communicate and understand your expectations (reasonable and otherwise) with your friends, then you may be surprised by the potential of a friendship to evolve into something more intimate or more sexual or more emotionally bonding. Keep in mind that sex is only one of a million ways to express love. Underlying all motives and ulterior pursuits, there must be a firm commitment to simply being friends. The new adage should be: Intimacy with a friend means never having to break up, because you know that you're still friends the next day.

Alternative relationships are not easy or simple. They require rigorous communication skills and constant re-working and re-adjusting to manage these growing and evolving connections. They demand attentive reassurance, a kind of blind faith in Love, and an ability to learn in the face of tremendous challenges. They are a constant struggle to overcome jealousy and to work through the embedded socialization process that can predetermine or affect our perceptions of what we feel and how we feel.

These are not simple concepts to understand, let alone

fully come to grips with in the early stages of an open relationship. Alternative relationships allow you the right to make ethical decisions for yourself, based on what is ultimately right for you. What you do with your life and your body and your heart is your own personal choice. Yet, even as you are free to make those choices, you must also be constantly aware of your effect on others. Your choices do affect your partner and your lovers, and this is no small juggling act.

Confronting Jealousy

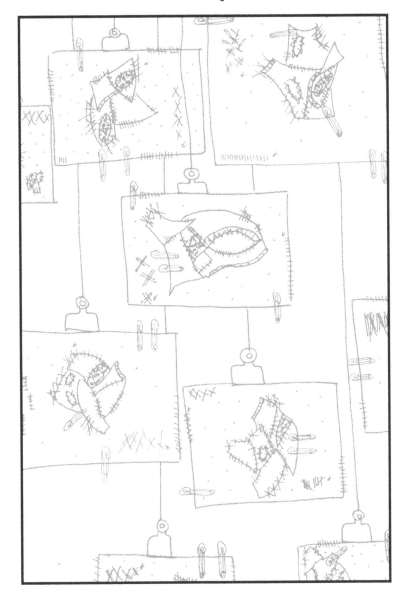

"Many people believe that sexual territoriality is a natural part of individual and social evolution, and use jealousy as justification to go berserk, and stop being a sane, responsible and ethical human being. Threatened with feeling jealous, we allow our brains to turn to static on the excuse that we are acting on instinct." Easton and Liszt, The Ethical Slut: A Guide to Infinite Sexual Possibilities

Confronting Jealousy

Jealousy is an ugly beast. Anyone who has ever experienced jealousy or been on the receiving end of it knows how threatening it is. It only pushes loved ones away and causes tremendous emotional damage to yourself and to others involved. Jealousy is also an emotion with which many people have had to grapple. However, it is how you deal with these feelings that will either make or break your relationship. Most of us, deep down, want to get past those feelings of jealousy, distrust, and rage. Confronting our issues of jealousy is a necessary and critical goal if you are planning to have an open relationship.

Establishing trust is the first order of business. Trust entails a commitment to yourself as well as with another person that you both can and will deal with anything that comes along. Sometimes this can be as easy as saying out loud to yourself or to another, "I can handle this. It may be hard or unpleasant right now, but I can handle it. I'm not scared." If you can ride out this storm, you are likely to find a strengthening of your commitment through the harder times.

One friend writes on the topic of jealousy:

"It can also be a grand opportunity for self exploration. I

see jealousy as a guidepost emotion. By honestly exploring what it is here that's making my stomach knot up in this special way, I always find a deeper understanding of myself and what I'm up to; generally with the added bonus of deeper connections and understanding with my partner(s). It's like peeling away the layers of an onion to get to what is really underneath it all. For example, I may be feeling jealous that my lover is out and about without me. However, upon closer examination, I'm feeling lonely and disappointed that my lover is not with me. In this light, it doesn't matter so much what my partner is out doing or with whom. What matters is that I have some work to do. I must fill my own loneliness by making the best of this time to be alone or by reaching out to friends. And that makes me powerful. I also get the chance to miss someone that I care to spend time with. This can turn controlling behavior into cherishing behavior. I can empower myself by creating solutions to my hurt feelings, unlike the dead-end that results from jealousy--where the one hurt is left only to blame and lash out."

Understanding Jealousy

Jealousy often symbolizes something else, beneath the surface. Examine and define this for yourself, get to the root of these feelings--like the layer of the onion analogy described above. Adopt new ways to manage your phases of jealousy. Reflect inward first, understand where these emotions stem from, then seek out reassurance (instead of blame) from friends or from your partner or from yourself. Take responsibility for your own feelings--they belong to you! This is the first step in self-acceptance. Invent creative ways to bolster your inner security, to have faith in the love and trust that you have for your partner. If you truly believe that you do not own your partner's body, then ultimately you must validate the love within yourself, for yourself, by yourself.

There's no way to really eradicate jealousy, but you can learn new routines to replace the old, negative paths that have led you only to more anger, pain, and scapegoating. Stop demanding that your partner or lover *prove* their love--the true test of love is loving yourself first. With practice, over time, you will gain self-control and a deeper understanding of yourself, instead of being continually sucked up into the tornado of jealousy. As one good friend put it, "Life presents challenges all the time--how we face them (or not) is our choice."

A non-jealous partner or lover also has a responsibility to listen, empathize, be supportive, provide reassurance, and to care. A non-jealous partner at times may feel tremendous guilt for the feelings expressed by a jealous partner, so part of your healing is being a part of their healing--they work hand in hand. A partner or lover who sticks by you through even the most difficult of times confirms their deeper acceptance and love for you.

Show how much you care, how much he or she means to you by validating their significance in your life. This might mean re-scheduling a date with another lover or a flower-run because your primary partner is having a mental breakdown. Make them feel that they're worth it to you. But keep in mind that you can only show them how you feel, you can't make a them feel a certain way.

Managing Jealousy

I find keeping a journal to be essential for managing a healthy course for my emotions, especially the negative ones. Poetry, painting, music, and introspection are positive and constructive outlets for jealousy, anger, disappointment, envy, and self-pity. Join a gym, go for a walk, ride your bike, take a hot bath; give your jealousy and pain an avenue to diffuse. Transfer pent-up rage and hurt into something rewarding. Don't punish yourself for being human. Give yourself the chance to learn and slowly change. Take care of yourself, nurture your emotions, cultivate the love from within, so others can plant more love around you.

Watch out for the tendency towards playing incessant head-games with yourself or with your partner when you feel jealous.

The truth is you don't know what goes on behind closed doors. There are platonic lovers, cuddle buddies, kissing friends, and love letter pen pals. Anguishing mental scenarios lead only to false accusations. You and your partner deserve fairer tactics. Head-games are ultimately damaging and re-confirm your own insecurities.

If you seek only love and meaningful connections in your life, then allow your partner the same freedom. Imagine your partner being the affectionate and loving friend that he or she is capable of being and deserves to be. You may never find yourself completely free of the tyranny of jealousy, but you can practice healthy coping mechanisms that will strengthen your overall understanding of the emotion and maintain stability within your relationships. The following steps are merely suggestive strategies for coping with jealousy.

Realizing this, I was quick to look for my own two feet. I would ache to feel them on solid ground. From my own base of operations, I could better get where I wanted to go and handle anything that came along. Upon arriving home, I had reached the center of the onion and found it was a real pearl. My pearl. Another hole plugged now, I didn't need him to be my anchor and I could get back to enjoying the pleasure of his company."

Early Stages

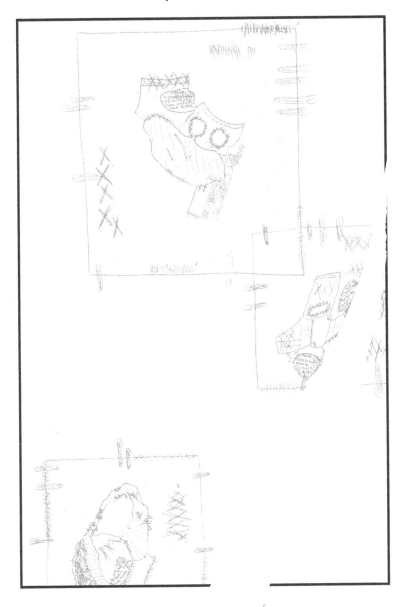

Early Stages

I strongly emphasize the importance of honest communication at the onset of a new connection. New relationships can grow in a number of directions, so think about what you really want from this person, what you are capable of truly giving, what your expectations are, and whether or not you are pursuing something more serious or less serious with them. Discuss this introspection with your new friend or lover and make the time to really sort through where you stand with each other in terms of the seriousness of your commitment in the short or long term.

Through my own personal experience, I recommend that for the first year or so of a serious relationship, couples may consider restraining from multiple outside lovers in order to lay the important groundwork of trust with your established partner. Setting up a solid foundation for a lasting relationship requires a lot of time. Limiting the number of deeply involved sexual partners is one way you can strengthen the bond between both of you in the early stages--so that when you finally do reach out to other lovers, you have something strong and resilient to fall back on. You and your partner have a sense of security, reassurance, and a deeper understanding of your role in each other's life.

Many will have to face their greatest fears around jealousy, possessiveness, control, and co-dependency that we are taught are perfectly acceptable in a "normal" relationship. Dissect your phobias, insecurities, and feelings of guilt. Examine where they come from, how and why they formed, and the situations that influenced your views on relationships. Many of us carry around fictionalized or false television-based concepts of a relationship.

In a healthy, ideal relationship, we need to foster inter-connectedness and learn to coexist while blending in our personal freedom to love and be loved. Cultivate the garden within first, before you branch out and nurture other gardens. Long-term couples can more easily ride through the havoc of emotions if the home base is secure and you both know you're standing on firm ground together.

How can you grow and come to love and trust someone, if you are off with someone else, particularly in the beginning of a serious relationship? A partially open relationship may be the only practical choice in the early stages of this kind of alternative relationship. The framework of a lasting connection gets built, little by little, until you naturally work to a point of openness of sharing lovers with your partner, or sharing sexual or intimate experiences apart. A partially open relationship may entail some restraint on your intimacy levels with new lovers. For example, cuddling, kissing and love letters might be acceptable, but sex or being gone for 2-3 nights a week might not be acceptable, especially if you are living together.

Learn to deal with the reality and the nature of a relationship by actively practicing what your heart desires while at the same time allowing your partner to have his or her needs met in other ways--and not just physical needs but love, friendship, support, etc. There will be times when a partner will shut down, for whatever reason, and he or she will not be able to give. As painful as that may be, it has to be accepted. This is why we understand and even encourage our partner, lovers or friends to reach out to others.

The Buddy System

The buddy system is something we learned as children but often forget to employ later in life. Having a close friend outside your primary relationship or lovers ensures that you have someone to help you through the emotional times. Seek out comfort from other understanding friends; this is one of the most pivotal steps in acknowledging that one person cannot fulfill all our needs. We need different people in our lives for different interactions. Bring back the buddy system. We tend to rely on our partners for this one, but having other close friends that you can share your weakest times with is crucial to healing and getting out of emotional ruts. Turning to others for emotional support or comfort allows others to be there for you. When you take responsibility for your feelings, you instigate the first step towards learning, growing, and moving on. No one else can heal your pain, it belongs to you. Figure out what you need to get through it and move forward.

Guidelines

Guidelines

When you respect mutually agreed upon boundaries, you build the foundation of lasting trust, which is the key ingredient in an open relationship. This list is only meant to be a helpful beginning for the do and don'ts of alternative relationships for establishing trust. Every couple must decide for themselves their own guidelines in the beginning, in order to avoid issues of distrust and hurt feelings. Every friend or lover or partner will have different ideas on how to approach and establish personal boundaries, so approach this section as a work in progress.

• **Practice Safe Sex:** Be responsible for your body and the bodies you come in contact with; our lives depend on it.

• **Respect Space Boundaries:** Discuss with your partner what is acceptable and respectful physical contact with outside lovers, especially if you live in the same house or if you are sharing space with a partner. Talk about respectful intimate or physical contact boundaries when partners and lovers are in the same place (i.e., parties, shows, bars), so that you will be able to draw the line should the occasion arise. For example, when your partner and your lover are at the same party, it may be perfectly acceptable to hug and hang out with both of them, but be considerate of how your actions and overt displays of affection may make either of them feel.

Designate neutral territory and safe or sacred space that you both agree upon. For example, consider places that are off limits to outside lovers for sex (i.e., partner's bed, house, car).

• **The "24-Hour" Rule:**   This rule came into effect when my primary partner and I agreed that you couldn't possibly know someone very well in less than 24 hours. We both agreed that there were far too many issues to discuss and to come to terms with before leaping in the sack with someone you don't know very well. I recommend that you take your time before getting too intimate with someone new without having sufficient time to get to know them, for them to get to know you, and to fully explain your relationship parameters. It is only fair to be honest with a new lover from the get-go and to not mislead them into falsely believing that your primary relationship is almost over and they are next in line, or that you are looking for another primary. It is only fair that a new lover have time (days, maybe weeks) to decide if they even want to get involved with you.

• **Honesty:**   This goes for all new lovers about your relationship situation as well as with your current partner. Honesty should not be confused with brutal insensitivity. For example, "I'm sorry I didn't get your call; I didn't have my pager on me," as opposed to, "My pager was in my pants which were on the floor as I was fucking so and so." There are loving ways to communicate what you choose to do with your life without being insensitive to your partner's feelings and insecurities. Ultimately, we are sensitive creatures, so it is important to pay attention to the words you choose, the people you spend time with, and the decisions you make.

No lies. Don't hide other friendships, lovers or partners. You might not reveal all the details of every relationship, but never hide where you go, who you're with, or when you'll be back. Once you start down that path of lies, you only dig yourself into deeper mistrust in the future.

- **Reassurance and Communication:** All partners, lovers, friends, and casual cuddle buddies deserve reassurance and communication time. Exercise the active listener in you. What bothers you or seems like a concern should be communicated before it festers into something loaded with resentment and insecurities. Don't hold things on people. Keep your connections clean. Learn how to ask for reassurance. Don't expect someone else to read your mind. Set aside special time for your needs or issues or concerns to be addressed. The ten minutes before they are out the door for work should not be the designated time to have that heartfelt talk. Make time for hurt feelings, listen, be loving, resist getting defensive, be comforting, and be willing to hear their pain. Discuss with your partner what is comfortable to do with others and what you may want to reserve to do with each other. Never invalidate the feelings of a partner.

Whenever conceivably possible, take your time and make wise choices--not hormone-crazed ones. Talk about risk factors, sexual history, sexually transmitted diseases, prior rape or abuse issues, sexual restrictions, what you can and can't handle physically or emotionally, and what things trigger your insecurities or fears. If you don't like one-night stands, be clear about this. Sex is not about conquest. Be up-front from the start. Granted, none of us admit full disclosure of our situation to someone we've only had a ten-minute conversation or flirtation with. Designate an appropriate time to have "the talk." New lovers have a right to know if you're "available," and what this availability entails, restricts, permits. It is important to be clear about intentions, motivations, and what you want out of this newly forming connection.

Timing is everything! Find a time when you and your lover are both available to talk and are in a good mood. The time to have that talk is not when you're stressed out, or at a party, or you've just made love.

Learn to make love through communication. Take the time to improve your verbal (and even written) skills. It will surprise you how powerful words can touch, stroke, caress and fondle without ever making physical contact.

• **Drugs/Alcohol:** Critical decisions regarding sexual intimacy with a lover are best made with a clear mind and an open heart, not a swirling, soggy brain. Think about how many sloppy decisions you've made under the influence. Ask yourself how it would feel if your partner made intimacy decisions while under the influence.

• **Motives:** Pursue friendship and love first. A large part of what makes open relationships work, in my opinion, is that you know in your heart that all relationships are, first and foremost, in the pursuit of friendship and loving connections. Personal motives and hormones need to be kept in check, especially if you are a very sexual person or a big flirt or you crave constant physical contact with others.

• **Privacy:** Never brag about other private, intimate connections to your partner or other lovers. Your individual experiences with all lovers are Private. Not every partner or lover wants to hear or can handle emotionally the details of your affairs. What you share and don't share about the physical attraction or the sexual content of your relationships is something you and your partner or lovers should discuss beforehand.

• **The "Bed-Hopping" Rule:** Try to avoid bed-hopping, emotionally and physically, between lovers and your partner. Make sure you have had ample time to process your emotions, wade through feelings, and then move forward in other directions. Bed-hopping can create emotional confusion. At the risk of sounding obvious, take a shower between lovers, wash your mind and body of another sacred place and person; write a love letter; go for a walk and clear your thoughts before returning to the home (or bed-side) of your partner's embrace. It is the thoughtful gesture that they deserve and truthfully, you want to be fully present when you are with someone you love.

• **Revise and Re-Define All Boundaries Regularly:**
Frequently review your boundaries, add new ones, modify old ones. Partners, friends, and lovers must commit to discussing regularly whether these boundaries are working or if new ones need to be added or altered. As relationships evolve so do our needs--our boundaries should reflect this evolution. Don't be defeated by what countless others seem to think. Make your own choices.

• **Treat Others as You Wish To Be Treated.**

• **Leave a Note:**   At the risk of sounding trite, if you live with a partner, always leave a note or call and leave a message when you anticipate that you might not come home at night. We are creatures of habit, if our partner doesn't come home, we will worry. Spare your partner the emotional crisis of wondering if you are alive and call, regardless of the time. With practice, it becomes second nature, and you will be relieved in the long run to know that they are o.k. Always leave a number where your partner can reach you, especially if you live together. You have a responsibility to your partner. This means a commitment to your future together. If you take this seriously, then leaving them a number gives them permission to reach you in case of an emergency or for reassurance or something truly important. Ultimately, you want to be available to your partner for anything of importance.

• **Never Act Out of Anger:**   Never act out against a partner or lover in anger or vengeance by sleeping with someone else.

• **Sharing:**   If you are both attracted to the same person, either share or find a comfortable way to keep it separate without making anyone choose. From the beginning, make a firm commitment to not letting this come between you and your partner.

• **Cuddle Companions:**   There is no such thing as too many cuddle buddies.

• **Sex, Sexual Contact, and Consensual Intimacy:**
   All sexual experiences are sacred. Find the right time to discuss your boundaries around all aspects of sexual conduct, be it as innocent as hugging and kissing to intercourse and oral sex. There may be things you only do with your primary partner and not your lovers, or the other way around. Decide what experiences may not be shared for now, discuss what is reasonable to ask of a partner and what will take more time to adjust to.

One bi-sexual woman writes:
   "My boyfriend still has issues with me being sexual with other guys. We don't want to end our relationship over this one issue, so I have agreed to only be sexual with women. I can still snuggle, kiss and be as affectionate as I would like to with men, but I understand that he is still trying to battle his jealousy for now. We will come back to this issue some time down the line and reassess how it's working out. The process of redefining boundaries and re-examining our relationship is an on-going discussion for us."

   I am a firm believer in the right to love anyone, anywhere, anytime, anyhow, but even loving connections have boundaries on intimacy. These "red flag" instances include intimacy or sexual contact with close friends or acquaintances of your partner or other lovers. Under these scenarios, be cautious--even a casual step in this direction can cause undue stress, misunderstanding, and severe (even irreversible) damage between you and your partner. Set boundaries around certain people that you and your partner feel would jeopardize your relationship. My partner and I try, whenever possible, not to get involved with overly jealous people, because we have dealt with the drama that comes along with it. Some couples may need boundaries around, for example, band members, best friends, roommates, or family members.

The heart may think it knows best, but I highly recommend communication and prior consent from your partner before acting out your desires with someone new. This is the time for patience and really thinking through your desires; consider the consequences of your actions. Ask yourself how you would feel if your partner got together with your best friend. And maybe it would hurt at first, maybe it would feel awkward the first couple of times you hung out with your best friend, maybe you would feel threatened that your partner and best friend would talk about you, maybe you secretly envy your partner's choice in lovers, or maybe the extended family ties of love and connectedness would bring everyone closer together in some unfathomable and magical way.

• **You Belong to Yourself:**   No one can own another person. You are not sexual property to be fenced in, controlled or monitored. No one can hold another person's body or love under lock and key. The ultimate goal of an open relationship is to love without possessing another person.

One woman writes:

"I may not approve of my partner's choices, which I'll certainly let him know, but he's free to do what he wants with or without my permission. I view this as another way we wield power over others. If it's someone I object to, my partner takes that into consideration but makes his own choice."

• **Rivals Are Not Allowed:**   One friend's suggestion: "It is important not to get involved in situations where two people may be pitted against each other. Anyone who cannot accept the place of your primary as Primary in your life should be dealt with caution. This may mean avoiding becoming too involved with someone who could challenge your feelings for your primary partner or someone who cannot accept the limits of your involvement with them. I would not, could not, get intimately involved with anyone unable to accept my partner as a vital and special component of my life."

• **Practice Loving Yourself:** Loving yourself first fosters your self-esteem. Make a pact with yourself that you will always work on loving yourself versus making someone else responsible for your feeling loved. Actively committing to nurturing, loving, and looking after yourself is the first step to building one's self confidence. For example, I love myself by soaking in a hot bath after a stressful day and going to great lengths to pamper myself head to toe. I love myself daily by eating healthy foods, taking care of my aches or illnesses, being good to myself, giving myself the tenderness I deserve, and exercising at the gym. Self-love is defined differently by everyone, so get creative on this one.

Conflict Strategies

I have some generally helpful suggestions in re-thinking how we approach conflict. Early on, my partner and I agreed that we are not capable of positive resolutions when we are in the heat of conflict or misguided by anger. We choose to wait until the negative emotions diffuse before we put aside quality time to discuss our issues. Nothing ever gets resolved when we're in a bad mood or when we're fighting the rest of the world. Avoid accusations like "you always" or "you never," articulate your own feelings, always make up, apologize and mean it, embrace afterwards, and practice letting go of the anger. Validate each other's feelings even if you disagree--this is not the time to get defensive. Verbalize and qualify your feelings with "I feel" and "this feels," instead of "you make me feel."

The 50-50 Rule

My partner and I practice the "50-50 Rule" which applies to responsibility, problem solving, and compromise. When a conflict arises, we will put aside time to talk about what is bothering us. We will follow the techniques mentioned above, and then we both agree to 50 percent of the resolution. This sounds easier than it is, because most of us come to an argument thinking we're right. But the 50-50 rule means we are each half responsible for what's wrong and half responsible for making it work and half responsible for coming up with solutions for our end of it. For example, we often end disagreements with one of us saying, "I will try harder to alleviate your fears about losing me and I will work on being a better listener because I understand how you feel." The other might follow with, "On my end, I will bring up my insecurities sooner instead of repressing them and causing stress on our relationship. I will give you the benefit of the doubt next time and trust that you were busy or forgot to call."

My partner and I find that following up every argument with "I'm sorry" and a hug usually breaks down our walls of resentment and anger.

Agree to Disagree

Most of us are taught to approach disagreements in a goal-oriented fashion (e.g. winners and losers). By this I also mean that each of us have, as an ultimate goal, to resolve our conflict. Unfortunately, what I have come to learn over the years, is that this form of thinking is too simplistic and leads to discouragement. The truth is, often, that the issue in conflict may never be fully resolved. There are times when we must agree to disagree. For example, there are reoccurring concerns between my partner and I that still have not been resolved, and that has to be okay. No two people are going to agree on everything. The lack of a final solution doesn't mean that you've failed in the relationship. Agreeing to disagree simply means acknowledging that you both tried to communicate about something important to you, but that time there has been no final conclusion. This also means the issue will resurface again in the future and hopefully you have had time to rediscover a more creative solution.

Challenge yourself, test yourself. What may seem like an impossible emotion to overcome (e.g. jealousy, fear of loss), may turn out to be not as *deadly* as you thought. Learn to experience emotions and fears as a sensitive being with time to process, and not as a maniac who feels out of control. Change and compromise are inevitable. There is no steering around it, but there are creative ways to manage miscommunications and misunderstandings. With practice and patience as your guide, conflict becomes a healthy and normal course of relationships, where we ultimately learn more about ourselves and our loved ones.

Acceptance

My partner once said to me, after a heated disagreement, "To love you, I have to accept the *whole package.*" And it's become our mantra. We're not together so we can force each other to change or to be someone that we're not. There may be parts of each other's personality or viewpoints or character-flaws that might trigger anger or disagreement. But each person comes as a whole package, based on unique characteristics and perspectives. Creative couples must find ways to cherish the good parts along side the not-so-good parts. The point is, to not let each other get swallowed up in the rage, dwell on your differences, and overlook your commonalities.

Life is about taking risks, crossing the line into the mystery of love with unknown variables and unreliable consequences. Truthfully, is there really such a thing as playing it safe when it comes to emotions? A person in an open relationship should not blame all their problems on the openness of that relationship. Relationships fail. Open or monogamous, married or casual lovers, failure happens. It's a fact of life. Monogamy is no guarantee that a partner won't cheat or leave you for someone else. Non-monogamy is no guarantee that your partner may find someone else. Some people will give others grief; some people may hassle a person about their choice to be non-monogamous--the problem may not necessarily be attributed to the form of relationship they've chosen. Take away the openness component and the negative person will find something else to fault. Non-monogamy is neither a solution to all of life's problems nor the cause of all that person's problem.

Some of Us Have Kids

The following chapter is an outside contribution by Famous. I was fortunate to have a friend take the time to write about her experience with open relationships and raising a child.

Some of Us Have Kids

A number of years ago, around the age of twenty-three, I found myself losing a man I was very much in love with. I was pretty oblivious to the fact that he was unhappy until he stopped coming home. One day I went out to find him comfortably camped out with an old friend. Needless to say, it ruined my relationship with her, but he and I attempted reconciliation. We managed another half year, though I didn't trust him and didn't feel I could let him out of my sight. It got so bad that I remember thinking I should make myself a sign for the inside of my door reminding me of my agenda for the day: Control and Possess. It was awful. I spent all my time trying to own him instead of loving him. We finally did part ways, but a lot of damage had been done not only to each other but to much of the community around us. It took a long time for me to sort things out, but I was sure it was going to be different the next time around. No more quests to possess, no more tests to prove love and devotion, no more rifts with my sisters.

After some time, I came to the conclusion that the best way to address some of my personal issues around possession and jealousy was to explore open relationships. For a while this meant keeping things casual, staying free to pursue any fancy as well as allowing anyone I was with a wide berth to also pursue any fancy. I learned a lot, but it wasn't until I started to fall in love with someone again and considered making commitments that the philosophies and principles of an open relationship began to flesh out in practical forms.

This relationship went well for a couple of years until I became pregnant. My partner and I came to understand that as we plot a course outside the status quo, all that we do can be new and different, occupying the realm of the alternative, until these practices are taught to another as Truth. Nowhere does this happen more effectively than when beliefs and principles are passed on to a child. Parents are in the position to present their version of the world as a matter of fact--a daunting, yet exciting, responsibility.

One of the first conclusions I came to with my partner was that it is important to keep the politics of parenting separate from the politics of being lovers. Being a mother or father really has nothing to do with being in love with the same person forever. With this goal in mind, the latitude afforded by keeping our relationship open, seemed to us, the most reliable and flexible flight plan with which to navigate the nebula of future possibilities. An open relationship can grow and evolve in a multitude of directions over time. Nowhere have I experienced a greater demand to grow and evolve than in the domain of parenthood. We had to re-evaluate almost all of our expectations, definitions, and commitments regarding our partnership and reassess our boundaries. More than ever, boundaries needed to be clearly defined and respected.

Pregnancy was a unique and profound experience wrought with emotions. Even under the best circumstances, there lie uncertainties, insecurities and revelations warranting close introspection. These aspects need to be shared and explored. A lot happens in those nine months. For some of the same reasons as in the early stages of a new relationship, it seems like a good time to restrain from multiple outside lovers. Not only is this period crucial to building trust, but a plethora of new concerns present themselves. For example, sexual health carries heavier consequences. The mother-to-be takes on more weight as well, and she may feel crazy. Unpredictable, surging hormones and an expanding waistband are difficult to handle. The playing field changes too. A woman with child may feel sexier than ever, but, then again, she may not. In addition, no amount of jealousy management may ease a partner's mind at the thought of an outside lover penetrating so near their child.

This is a special and particular episode in your lives together. If everything about your relationship is different at this time than at any other time, it wouldn't at all be surprising. I needed to ask my partner to be monogamous for a while. If monogamy is not your choice, anyone involved at this time should thoroughly examine their role and commitments in the formation of a new family. This is prime-time to shore up your relationship(s) in preparation for glorious but tough times to come. Any holes will be blown wide open under the stresses of the tighter interconnectedness that accompanies co-parenting. You are both in transformation. You are fast approaching a new level in the emotional terrain. Respect and honor this time.

Once our baby arrived, it came time to re-negotiate again. The first year or two were crucial in building a strong, trustworthy foundation to last a lifetime--our daughter's lifetime. Raising a child together engenders shared responsibility, and that creates an interdependency that leaves less room for simple discretion. We found ourselves confronting things about ourselves and each other that we never expected. We were living in closer quarters, sharing a home and in constant communication regarding the daily maintenance of a child.

The time constraints were sometimes unbelievable. In the first few years, a child demands almost constant attention. I needed attention, my partner needed attention, our relationship needed attention. Add to this time spent on a job, chores (we found we had more laundry in a week than we used to in a month), sleeping, and eating. This doesn't even approach fitting in a social life. It was impossible to find time away to just "do our own thing." Still, we managed to open things back up.

For us, the period of monogamy did not need to continue much past our baby's arrival, but we were acutely aware that we were floating in a different boat. No more going out for the afternoon and coming home a day later, because that would leave one person holding the bag on a shared responsibility. Whoever was alone with our baby was very much aware of the other's absence. My time with our baby was less my time as it was hers. Try sorting out something heart-wrenching when there is a little one in need of attention. In effect, any activity outside raising our baby required familial support whether it be work, school, a solo trip to the museum or a visit with other lovers. However, even as we talked about resuming our extracurricular affairs, it was a bit awkward putting that into practice after a period of respite.

The first time for us was like this: we were at a party and our baby was home with a sitter. One of us had to go home at a decent hour and since I'm the sleepy-head in the family, I was ready to go home first. I asked him to come with me, but I knew at the time I just wanted the familiar company until I got home and into bed. After that, I didn't mind what was on his agenda. I also figured that I wasn't missing as much if he was home with me missing it all too. Naturally, he wasn't ready to leave, so I walked home, crawled into bed and reveled at all the room I had to stretch out. I woke up in the morning, however, and it was still just me and the baby. Instead of "hooray," it was more like, "I wonder what this means?"

He did eventually come home to tell me what it meant. He called to let me know he was on his way, and did I want anything. He brought me a bagel and made a date with me to talk. I may have wanted to get into it then and there, but he already had obligations for the day. I held out till later, because he really did all the right things along the way. He put forth the effort to let me know he was accessible, I would get the explanations I needed, and all the while, expressing this attitude that it was all okay. It was okay that he spent the night away. It was okay that I would have feelings regarding such and it was okay that he would need to address them with me. This was all reassuring behavior on his part: "I'm on my way home, I'm thinking about you, I'll be there to sort things out with you soon." If he was not freaked out about any of this, I didn't need to freak out either.

I spent the day collecting my thoughts and feelings, and the evening expressing them to my partner. There were things I needed to cry about, things I needed to ask why about, things I needed to ask if I should worry about. I did not need to blame, accuse or wail. I listened and accepted his reassurances. This left us feeling closer to each other and stronger in our commitments both to each other and our way of loving each other. Perhaps we could sail out into uncharted waters with our little babe in tow and find our way.

Now, it was a different challenge the other way around. Being home-bound as a result of breast feeding for two years, it was clear that for an in-depth outside relationship to occur, it would have to be in our home. This meant my partner would have to contend with (though perhaps not engage with) my other interests by at least knowing they would be coming around.

He actually took the first step in making this dynamic okay and workable. Someone he had met the previous summer while traveling was in town visiting. Someone who, it was not hard to imagine, would peak my interest. He needed a place to stay for a couple of nights and my partner invited him home. My partner let me know very simply that this was a person he trusted and was comfortable with and that, although he wasn't going to give up his spot in our bed at night, he would be at work all day and how ever our guest and I wanted to spend our time together was up to us. I was nearly overwhelmed by the amount of understanding and grace my partner exhibited at that time. I really needed some reassurances from sources other than the one who, of course, had to find me fun and desirable because he loved me. I needed to flirt and giggle with someone who found me attractive just meeting me as I was (which, at this time, I was settling into my third body type/shape in less than two years and I had a lot of questions regarding how I felt about it). In addition to bringing a lover home for me, my partner helped me figure out how I was going to cope with my very new and different circumstances.

So that is some of how it was for us, but I have also had a lot of time to reflect on how it must be for our daughter to grow up with a different frame of reference for relationships. In the context of a radical, open relationship, children can be exposed to a wide range of loving behaviors. Little ones are creatures of love, so it seems invaluable to rear them in such a way that they grow up knowing that there is more than one place to get a hug, support, encouragement, a sympathetic ear, or undivided attention. I don't mean to imply that this dynamic comes about just because there are other lovers around, but because open hearts foster an assortment of meaningful connections. We used to have extended families in which to get our varied emotional exercises. As this paradigm fades from our collective memories, it seems beneficial to bring as many allies as possible into the family fold.

The way in which we incorporate others into our family life allows our baby to see others not as rivals for mom or dad's attention, but as another person who could help her reach the fruit bowl or read a book or dress up her dollies. In this way, she stays open to people and looks for what is special about them as well as what she may be able to share with them. Our daughter is always asked what she thinks of a possible new roommate situation and her feelings are truly considered. I have not sensed jealousy on her part except where she is feeling excluded. Isn't that the case for many of us?

An example more particular to a non-monogamous home: I was seeing someone I liked quite a bit, but he was very busy during the daytime. This often meant he wasn't coming around until late, usually after our daughter was asleep. She would wake up in the morning to find this person camped out in her house. She wasn't too keen on the idea that things were obviously going on after she was out for the night, especially things involving someone as close to her as her mother. In this instance, my late-night lover was encouraged to come around during "kid hours" to play and read books, even if only for a brief amount of time. If he couldn't find the time for this accommodation, he couldn't sleep over. I'm sure similar things have happened to many of us. We turn in early one night only to wander out early the next morning in our underwear and trip over people we don't know in the living room. I generally don't warm up to them until I am properly introduced.

When our daughter indicates she doesn't like someone or some situation, we don't write her reactions off as "just jealous." We explore what it is she doesn't like. Maybe her and another person or situation don't mix well, but often it is the case that some boundary of hers was overlooked or is newly formed and needs to be incorporated into our list of agreements. When these things come up, we, as her parents, understand that it is our work to help her decipher her feelings and make her more comfortable with the dynamics of a home that we all share. Because it is not her job to change her feelings or adopt adult coping mechanisms, it is our job to help her get to the root of her unease and figure out what we can do to address them. My partner and I are again called out to negotiate, define and respect boundaries just as we do for each other. In this way, not only are we teaching our daughter the art of peeling away the layers of that onion we call jealousy, but also that her feelings and opinions are important, listened to and worthy of attention. How many of us graduates from the school of, "children are to be seen and not heard", are still struggling, nagging, wailing and screaming because no one has ever validated our feelings and opinions as important?

Sometimes, however, relationships don't work out. You

may do all the good and healthy things you can possibly do and it may appear that this partnership will only go on forever, but it doesn't. One of the unexpected benefits of an open relationship was brought to fruition when my partner and I had to part ways. Never an easy task, but throw a kid, a house, a car and a joint bank account into the mix, and it seems next to impossible. Luckily, I was able to see our relationship as evolving instead of breaking. This was a comfort lacking in previous partings. Having been pathetically devastated in the past, I certainly wanted to avoid the anguish of losing my lover-partner-best friend-entertainment while at the same time coping with single parenting. The evolutionary possibilities fostered by an open partnership paid off with the ability to paint an unconventional family portrait once mom and dad didn't want to live together anymore.

Thankfully, we've been able to skirt many of the usual issues around parents splitting up. For example, not only were he and I accustomed to seeing each other with other people, so was our daughter. So far, we have not detected any sense of jealously in our daughter regarding new friends, lovers or housemates. She is free to meet and greet anyone more on her own terms. Since we have always been affectionate with the folks we care about, our daughter need never be concerned with whether the people around mom or dad are friends or lovers. Just that they are quality. This way she foregoes some of the anxieties traditionally experienced by children of divorced parents. She need not worry about anybody being replaced by another, or having to protect anyone's feelings by not mentioning who her mom's dinner companion was yesterday, or being in the position to report on another's activities. These are complex issues for an adult, much less a child who should really just be worrying about who they want to play with today. My current goal is to create a relationship which allows our daughter's family to grow and expand as opposed to becoming separate and disjointed. In this way, perhaps she will never have to choose between families.

Although it has not been my experience, it is not hard to

envision drawbacks when open relationships are not handled responsibly and maturely--this is fertile ground for mistrust and insecurities. Boundaries need to be clearly expressed and respected. Responsibility is compounded when there is a child involved. Commitments are written in ink not pencil.

We try to stay aware of the fact that we are chiseling out a version of the way things ought to be and passing it on to a whole new generation. While we're at it, we figure some good, solid conflict survival skills would be just the thing to pass along as well. There have been times when the man I share a child with and myself have not been able to agree on anything. But bearing in mind the welfare of our daughter has compelled us both to develop and employ conflict strategies that promote resolution. In efforts to shield our daughter from screaming matches, there were times when we had to write each other letters in order to discuss the issues that we were having. Other times we would agree to get together after our daughter was asleep to hash out various tribulations. We would also practice not trashing the other person in front of our daughter and speaking of each other in positive terms in relation to our child.

Reassuring behaviors towards our daughter are invaluable in tough times, such as: "I know you miss mom/dad. They aren't here right now, but that's okay because you're going see them soon. Besides, we get to hang out and have fun." When parents engage in behaviors that hurt and disrespect each other, a child absorbs all that psychic garbage. When parents engage in behaviors that support and consider each other, a child may frolic in a rich emotional garden. There is no way to predict all that you and your partner(s) will face. Just start at the beginning and keep talking. What are the commitments you need to make to each other? How do you want to involve how many people in your family life? What kind of relationship paradigm do you want your kid(s) to inherit? What does your version of family look like?

Life as Options

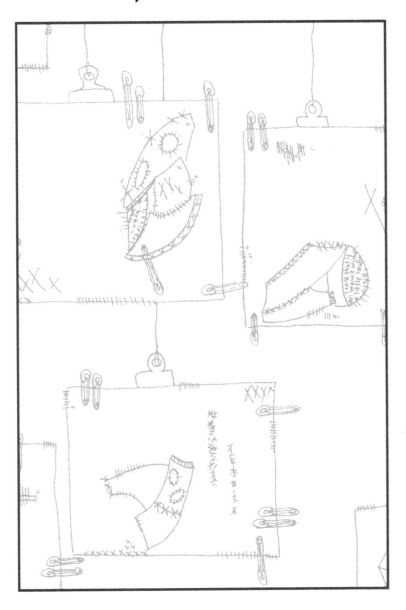

"Imagine what it would feel like to live in an abundance of sex and love, to feel that you had all of both that you could possibly want, free of any feelings of deprivation or neediness. Imagine how strong you would feel if you got to exercise your "love muscles" that much, and how much love you would have to give!" Easton and Liszt, <u>The Ethical Slut: A Guide to Infinite Sexual Possibilities</u>

Life as Options

Some relationship scenarios are often feared and avoided by even the most adventurous individuals and couples. In this lies our greatest challenge--how do we construct new relationship models that will survive the test of time and love? There is no guarantee that a situation might work itself out for the best, but there is inherent truth and great wisdom from even the most painful of consequences. I can honestly say that I have no regrets about the pain, because it is a part of life that we cannot avoid. I ask you: what truly mind-blowing relationship has ever been safe?

Both my partner and I have been in love and involved with outside lovers. On no occasion has the love I have felt for someone else conflicted with or weakened my love for my primary partner. Though we have imagined and feared a scenario that would cause us to part ways, we believe that our love was meant to be shared and that we can only grow from our experiences with others.

At one time we had a woman live with us, a lover to both of us. We once experienced a jealous outside lover try to come between us. We have both expressed our apprehensions or distrust about certain selected friends or lovers, but we have never stood in the way or withheld trust for each other's decisions. We talk openly about our fantasies and have savored the chance to try new things and new people. Together we have learned when it is comfortable to push boundaries and experiment, and when it is not. Sometimes we just ask, "Are you okay with this?" or "Does this sound like fun?" or "How would you feel if we did this?"

Non-monogamy has also permitted me to commit to a relationship with my best friend that would not have reached the depth of emotion and intimacy had we both been in restrictive or possessive relationships. My relationship with her would most certainly have been a threat to our other lovers if we had not been free to explore a more ground-breaking connection. Twelve years later, we are deeply in love, and despite being platonic, we have found countless ways to express our love and commitment. She is as much my soulmate and lover as my partner.

Non-monogamy lends itself to the type of situation where one partner travels for extensive periods of time. Having an open relationship to explore loving connections while they're gone prevents the partner at home from feeling resentful and lonely. Practice forming a body of friendships and alliances that cover a broad spectrum of supportive ties.

One man writes:

"Here's some examples of open relationships that I've been in. Some of these experiences were better than others, and I learned a lot about people and about myself from each of these scenarios.

"As a young man, I was involved with an older woman who introduced me to the idea of non-monogamous relationships. As a lover of freedom and someone who felt stifled by traditional relationships, I was intrigued. We agreed that we would both see other people and made an effort to communicate our thoughts and feelings about it as we went along. Things went well for some time until my lover slept with my best friend in the bedroom next to mine. I tried to be cool but I was going nuts as I listened to them having sex next door. I was afraid it would be uncool to tell them that I was hurt by this action and I decided that maybe I was not cut out for this type of relationship. I blamed myself but I was wrong. It was years later that I figured out that the key to successful open relationships is freedom and responsibility. Not freedom from responsibility.

"So I decided to give it another go with a woman I was involved with who was also into the idea. In the beginning, long before sleeping with outside lovers, we talked about it quite a bit. We laid out certain ground rules and let each other know what our expectations and limitations were. Some of our rules were: 1) no sleeping with best friends!; 2) we agreed not to discuss the details of our sexual relationships with other lovers (although some people are into this!); 3) we agreed to let each other know when we would be gone and for how long; and 4) we promised to talk about it at any time if either of us felt uncomfortable. It was, after all, about love. We wanted to help each other grow as individuals, and to live and love to our fullest potential. We hit some rough spots but for the most part we were very happy. We acted responsibly and treated each other respectfully. We often knew each others lovers and sometimes interacted socially with them. (Although we also found it helpful to find lovers outside of our social group or even geographic area.) Everything was completely above board, our other lovers and friends were aware of our situation and many were inspired by it. It did take some work, but any worthwhile relationship does, and it was well worth it! I think we are both more complete people because of it.

"Currently, I'm in a different kind of non-monogamous relationship, which is considered unconventional even by the standards of anarchists or other practitioners of open relationships. My girlfriend and I operate under what is commonly called the "don't ask-don't tell" policy. We don't live together, and we are happy with this arrangement. My lover and I have an implicit understanding that it's okay for us to see other people, but we've agreed to spare each other the details. When we are together, we are focused on each other and we have a great time. When we're not together, we're each free to do whatever we want. We don't ask each other prying questions about our time apart. It doesn't matter! What's important is the time and love we share together. This arrangement has kept us happy for a long time.

"These relationships are not for everybody, but they may well be for you if you're reading this book! They are often hard work but anything worth having usually is. As you can see from the examples in this book, there's no one way to do it. Challenge yourself, respect yourself and those you love. Explore your capacity to love and have fun!"

Another man writes:

"My friend Mary has been in town and things have turned out better than I would have dreamed. The first month we were just platonic friends--hung out a lot, made music, talked. I just let her go at her own pace. One night she opened up emotionally with me and appreciated that I was able to just be her friend. I explained that I was interested in her but not letting that get in the way of our friendship. A few more days passed and we finally made love. Things have been very natural and it's been beautiful. It's been a long time since I've had three days in a row where all you do is make love with somebody and go to your jobs. I totally love this woman.

"Another beautiful part of this whole experience has been the fact that a few months prior, I started hanging out with this woman Jane. She's another amazing radical-feminist-gardner-vegan-baker-anarchist-land-loving-fun-strong-independent-herbalist woman. Jane and I have had a non-monogamous situation from the start--we've both had other lovers. What's completely cool is Mary and Jane have become really great friends--they hang out together on their own and Jane has turned out to be one of Mary's closest female friends.

"The three of us will hang out together as well, and it's becoming more and more comfortable each time. Once in a while

I will feel a little nervous--so I just act more as everybody's friend in those situations. Each of us knows and accepts the relationships we've formed separately. But it's been intense for me getting in this deep--a loving and intensely physical friendship/relationship with Mary while also being in a really wonderful but definitely more relaxed situation with Jane. I also feel good about this situation since they are both women whom I admire and respect completely, and who can also be friends with each other."

Table II

How to Share a Lover with Your Partner

Do & Don'ts
• Do not bring home a lover to share with your partner before clearing it with them first.

• If you and your partner agree to share a lover, no matter what your expectations may be, it has to be okay for anyone involved to change their mind without pressure or consequences. Keep your disappointment to yourself.

• The time to talk about fears, concerns, worries, or to hash out any issues is before you get sexually involved.

• Be prepared and have a sufficient stock supply of condoms, lubrication, dental dams and safe-sex paraphernalia.

• Start off *slow* and don't be in a rush to get the orgasm. This is the time for extra reassurance and tenderness for all people involved.

Table II

How to Share a Lover with Your Partner

Do & Don'ts
• Be prepared emotionally for the unexpected. A lover or partner may experience jealousy or start to cry or feel overwhelmed or run out of the room with fear and anxiety. That's normal. It takes time to get used to new people and sharing someone intimately can be scary and unpredictable. It doesn't mean it was a bad idea, it simply means that we will experience our emotions as they arise and we have so much to learn as we go along.

• Learn to be a good cuddler and establish trust and patience first.

• Always remember to keep in close verbal contact with a shared lover before, during, and after. Often partners forget that the third person doesn't have the same ongoing buddy system to fall back on. Check in emotionally with outside lovers soon after lovemaking.

doubt. There may be days when you question the very foundation of your relationships and everything you believe in, but don't be misguided by rumors from outsiders. Let's face it, monogamy is no guarantee that people will like or dislike you. Choosing an open relationship means that even your friends may pass judgment and not agree or accept your alternative choice.

It's no wonder why so many of us are in the closet about non-monogamous practices. Learn to pick and choose carefully who you wish to disclose such information to. For me, this topic of "coming out" is a touchy one. While I can talk to my best friend and my sister about every detail of my love life, I am torn about being misunderstood by my mother, or by my in-laws, and even some of my friends. Though I have always been adventurous and I have frequently broken the socially accepted norms set down by our culture, there is no easy answer for facing your fears about being misunderstood by loved ones. Only you can decide with whom you will be open. Ultimately, I would like to reach a point where I am free to be who I am without needing anyone's acceptance. But for now, I'm just not there yet.

We live in a time where we can choose our sexual identity or decide for ourselves if we want to be religious or not. We can choose to have a live-in partner and never marry, and we can cho to have children or not. It is safe to assume that we also have a to decide if multiple relationships are more suitable to our lifes. It is time to stop letting society convince you that you should fe bad or guilty about how many people you choose to love. This ı our opportunity to form new households for the future and tc foster healthy and responsible relationships. There is nothing stopping you from finding the courage to love as many people as possible and inviting them to help you raise a family, form friendships with your children, live in separate rooms, share lovers, share laundry, set boundaries, and start a mini-revolution in the privacy of your own home.

Free-Writing Piece on Love

Free-Writing Piece on Love

I have met so many people who tell me that they don't know what love is or don't really believe it exists. And when pressed on the topic of love, they either have become disillusioned or jaded by past relationships, such that love has lost all meaning to them, or they find some way to turn it into a joke. Sometimes I think they've been hurt in the past and it is safer to build walls around their heart than to risk rejection again. I have done the same. Others have a vague sense of love for a family member or for a close friend (often platonic), or love for an inanimate object (e.g., guitar, stereo, book, motorcycle) that brings them immeasurable happiness.

I know for certain that we all have fears around the falling in love part because it requires taking emotional risks. It requires recognizing one's own expectations (reasonable or otherwise), and admitting desires, needs, wants, hopes. I know that love starts from within. You must love yourself first, wholly and entirely and daily, all faults and misgivings, all aspects, deformities, shortcomings, physically, emotionally, spiritually, and mentally. How you go about attaining this love or connection within yourself, with your soul (as you are the keeper and guardian of your soul alone), is different for everyone.

This is where creativity comes in handy. If you love yourself, then you'll do whatever it takes. You'll do crazy and bizarre things for yourself just to keep that love alive. It's like tending a campfire; we all have our own inner candle that goes out sometimes and needs re-fueling, re-kindling, or a jump start.

I know that sometimes, when people grow up without some of the essential ingredients and they aren't exposed to good role models of a loving relationship, they don't have a well-balanced understanding of what love is or could be. Our childhood experience will greatly shape how we perceive love and intimacy. Frequently, we are influenced by outside role models that are often fictitious, not based in reality, romanticized, or simply television-based. We have all experienced moments of romanticized versions of love or intimacy, but they don't usually last very long. Which isn't to imply that real love must last a defined amount of minutes, days, or years. Love cannot be simplified this way.

There is a tendency to want to put love in a tight frame, easily defined, and then put it on a shelf to over- or underanalyze. But love is far too clever to cooperate on this insignificant level. Love may park herself on a barstool and drink herself into denial. She may stumble aimlessly down a dead-end street, feeling lonely and sorry for herself, but you can't get rid of her that easy. She may fly around from bed to highway to river, but she can't be drowned. And she may go blind and lose sight of all the beauty around her, or go deaf and not hear the voices telling her how much they feel for her, or grow cold to the touch and not feel the impression of that last embrace, but she isn't dead yet.

Love just isn't fool-proof (or bullet-proof). She comes with hang-ups and miscommunications and people who give up easily when things get uncomfortable or when they get tired of always being the one to initiate everything. She comes with carefully implanted timing devices, and you can never predict her, which is exciting and challenging for some, frightening and discouraging for others.

You can't confine love to some ultimate act of selflessness or heroism, because love is also tricky and flighty and fickle and indecisive and far too human to fit into any single category. In fact, she dislikes categories of any kind, she demands to be set free, wild, untamed, unpredictable.

Inspiration is an outlet for love. When you have love for someone, you are inspired to do things for them, purely as an act of kindness and not because they owe you something in return. Love has no guarantees, no return-policy, no cash-back, no refunds, no price tag, no guidelines. That's what is so problematic about love. It's a wild ride on the beautiful side of life but completely in the dark. It's a catch-22; in order to have love, you must set her free, give it all away, give to yourself, and still there's no prepackaged directions or recipe or map to get you where you want to be.

Love is inherently the ability to accept whatever the outcome may be, because there is no outcome that is written in stone or that might still reverse itself five minutes or five years later. And love is not restricting one person to fulfill all your needs. You may be in love with only one person, but you must get other needs met by other people. It would be unfair and pressuring to make that one person responsible for all your happiness. "There's got be to more than one place to get a hug," as one friend points out. You've got to make yourself happy, so that anything else that comes along is simply the icing on the cake or the way they say your name that gives you that warm feeling or missing someone that you're thankful to have in your life or someone you know you can count on through even the most vulnerable and weakest of times or the funny outlook they have on life or their smell or the way you feel around them.

Love is easily satisfied by the smallest gesture or by the slightest moment of pleasure, because that's life.

Love is or it isn't, but you ultimately are responsible for it or the lack of it in your life. Love can get misplaced or misguided or even say all the wrong things at the wrong time, but she forgives easily. Love will definitely frustrate and confuse the hell out of you for what may seem like an eternity, but eventually she teaches us an important lesson about not losing faith in love or ourselves.

Love inspires us to be humble and generous and reminds us to leave our ego outside. Love begins, ends, begins, ends, starts off in the middle and then cuts you off at the pass. She flushes you down into the sewage of loneliness and self-loathing, and then kicks your ass when you least expect it. Love is available when you're not, and sentenced to life imprisonment when you're on the prowl again. She just doesn't quit, and neither can you.

See truly.
Live fully.
Think for yourself.

My Path

Let them dissect
my thoughts
They'll never find what they're after.
I feel the pull
the weight of a lie
heavy in my mouth
this full disclosure
I feel the pull
I want only freedom
without ownership
the door wide open
I want only love
in its limitless capacity
no fear of the unknown
I feel the pull
no one to hold me back
no one to tell me how to live
no one to block my path
"living my life," Emma reminds me again
to demand nothing less from myself
I am a force
that cannot be reckoned with.

Wendy-O Matik

(Dedicated to Emma Goldman)

Bibliography

Allison, Dorothy, *Skin: Talking about Sex, Class & Literature*. Firebrand Books, Ithaca, NY, 1994.

Anapolis, Dr. Deborah M., *Polyamory: The New Love Without Limits*. Intinet Resource Center, San Rafael, CA, 1997.

Easton, Dossie and Catherine A. Liszt, *The Ethical Slut: A Guide to Infinite Sexual Possibilities*. Greenery Press, San Francisco, CA, 1997.

King, Paul, *Polyamory: Ethical Non-Monogamy*, AlterNet.org, 2001.

Lano, Kevin and Claire Parry, ed., *Breaking the Barriers to Desire: New Approaches to Multiple Relationships*. Five Leaves Publications, Nottingham, England, 1995.

Starhawk, *The Fifth Sacred Thing*. Bantam Books, New York, NY, 1993.

Bibliographical Notes

Visit your local small press bookstore for titles on this subject. If you have access to the web, look up books on non-monogamy or other related topics. Read anything you can get your hands on. Some stuff will be outdated or not from your generation--read it anyway. Guidance and insight can come from the strangest places. Keep a journal of your own relationship history, experiences, advice, ideas, and values.

Suggested Topics for Further Analysis

• The role of early patriarchal Judeo-Christian religion in the ownership of women through the strict enforcement of monogamy and matrimony.

• Non-monogamous practices in Chinese, Indian, ancient Sumerian (now southern Iraq), Tibetan, Ceylon, Native American, African, Egyptian, Celtic, Roman and Greek cultures and mythologies.

• Modern society's obsession with monogamy as the dominant form of a relationship archetype.

• Primate sexual behavior and relationships in contrast with human sexual behavior (i.e. the bonobo chimpanzee).

• A resource section with magazines, periodicals, books, websites, workshops, support groups, organizations, hotlines, etc., on the topic of non-monogamy.

• The philosophy and/or politics of love, intimacy and sex.

• Case studies on multiple primary partners, polyfidelity, polyamory and non-monogamy.

• Domestic violence and conflict resolution.

• A how-to manual on loving yourself.

• The origins of jealousy as a purely socialized emotion or a remnant of our evolution.

• New definitions, "labels," and models for non-traditional relationships.

About the Author

Wendy-O Matik is a freelance writer and published poet in the Bay Area. She is a seasoned traveler and spokenword performer in the underground scene. She is available for educational and motivational discussions on the topic of alternative relationship models and responsible non-monogamy.

About the Artist

The cover page and chapter illustrations are the work of Erin Brookey. Erin's medium consists of her own undergarments, lingerie, safety pins, and journal entries, which are then carefully hand-stitched together and sealed in plastic. Her work is symbolic of our relationships--the stitching together of the scraps of who we are and what we are amidst our heartache and confusion. It represents the vulnerable, exposing ourselves, a revealing of our most private secrets, with also an element of detachment and impenetrability--that which we do not allow others to know, that which lies trapped behind the plastic. Sewing is both cathartic and at the same time represents reparation--like what the heart goes through with every break-up.

Notes

Orders

Redefining Our Relationships:
Guidelines For Responsible Open Relationships
by Wendy-O Matik
ISBN No. 1-58790-015-7

REGENT PRESS
Berkeley, California
www.regentpress.net
regentpress@mindspring.com

AK Press Distribution   Last Gasp
674-A 23rd Street   777 Florida Street
Oakland, CA 94612 USA   San Francisco CA 94110
Voice 510-208-1700   800-848-4277
Fax 510-208-1701   FAX 415-824-1836
info@akpress.org   gasp@lastgasp.com
www.akpress.com   www.lastgasp.com

Slug & Lettuce Book Distro
P.O. Box 26632
Richmond, VA 23261-6632
SASE for a catalog
chris1slug@hotmail.com

DEFIANT TIMES
PRESS
Oakland, CA

defianttimespress@lycos.com

CPSIA information can be obtained
at www.ICGtesting.com
Printed in the USA
FSHW021255030520
69658FS

9 781587 900150